HAPPILY
SEPARATING

THE OKUN/BILLIAN WAY
TO AN AMICABLE SPLIT
(AND OTHER LIFE LESSONS)

By Harvey L. Okun and
Alan L. Billian

authorHOUSE®

AuthorHouse™
1663 Liberty Drive
Bloomington, IN 47403
www.authorhouse.com
Phone: 1 (800) 839-8640

Published by AuthorHouse   12/17/2015

ISBN: 978-1-4969-0614-4 (sc)
ISBN: 978-1-4969-0615-1 (e)

Library of Congress Control Number: 2014907436

Print information available on the last page.

Contents

Foreword

If you are reading our book, you are likely going through a break up of some kind or are contemplating one. The content of this book - the stories, the advice, and life lessons - are the result of more than 50 years of combined legal experiences.

When reading this book, it is important to remember that while we advocate a conciliatory approach to the resolution of your domestic situation, a conciliatory approach does not always work. Sometimes it becomes necessary to seek court intervention and to litigate the resolution of your relationship. It is important to remember, when proceeding with litigation, to do so in a dignified and respectful manner.

There is nothing wrong with being passionate as this demonstrates the depth of your conviction. We are passionate for our clients both in and outside of the courthouse. The fact we are consistently told by judges to "calm down" demonstrates that our passion for our clients has never been questioned.

Writing this book to help you to "happily separate" has become a passion for us as well.

We want to thank our families, colleagues, clients, our Office Manager, Katie Lowman, and our business coach,

Mark Luterman, for their support in the publication of this book.

In reading this book, we hope that you will enjoy our stories[1] and take away a road map for your future success and happiness.

---

[1]   Names have been changed to protect client confidentiality.

Chapter 1

The Power of Forgiveness and Positive Thinking

Written by Harvey L. Okun

"When you are able to forgive, you release the negative energy that keeps you from thinking positive thoughts. Once you forgive, you move on to the second step and that is to forget. Many people forgive, but they can't forget. One cannot work without the other, which means you need to accomplish both to attain total emotional freedom." Napoleon Hill

Living a Healthier and Happier Life

Studies have shown that people who forgive are happier and healthier than those who hold resentment. The research of Dr. Fred Luskin of Stanford University and author of the book, <u>Learning to Forgive</u>, presents evidence that the process of forgiveness can be learned, and the effects of forgiveness are excellent for your mental and physical health. When people forgive, it leads to improved functioning in their cardiovascular and nervous systems.

Second Wife in Foreign Country

A young married lady came to see me when she discovered, through a very unusual means, that her husband was romantically involved with someone in a foreign country. Her sister received a wedding invitation from the husband's new bride to be. To further complicate the matter, the sister discovered that they actually had a ceremony, which the husband called a ceremony of love, and not a wedding ceremony, in a foreign country. The ceremony itself was on YouTube[2], so anyone who had access could watch it. Eventually my client actually saw the ceremony. It certainly looked like a wedding ceremony to her and me, but the husband, through his lawyer, continued to say it was just a ceremony of love. Our client was able to set aside these facts, and forgive her husband enough that they were able to resolve their property issues and to obtain an uncontested divorce.

Chutzpah

My client was the husband/father who found out that his wife was having an affair, and actually charged gifts on <u>his</u> credit card, including a motorcycle for her boyfriend. They have words for that, ranging from unmitigated gall, nerve, and the Yiddish expression "chutzpah." My client still had feelings for his wife, and since he was the far better parent, I was able to obtain primary physical custody for him. He forgave his wife and set aside his negative feelings about the affair, because he knew it was

---

[2]   What should be remembered in this case is the risk of putting yourself out there in any type of social media has become one of Divorce lawyers' favorite weapons. It is amazing to us how individuals disclose their most intimate details of their lives on social media websites such as Facebook. It is very easy now to access anyone's Facebook page to find incriminating evidence against the opposing party. Our advice to our clients is not to use social media sites during the entire separation process. You have a right to expect your attorney to keep everything confidential, but you also must exercise that same obligation yourself.

in the best interests of his children that they spend time with their mother.

Focus on the Future

In any breakup there are strong feelings that are present. The job of the attorney is to have his or her client focus on the future, not the past. It is important for the attorney to be able to teach the client that there is no point in focusing on the past.

We have a sign in our office that says, "It is what it is." You can't have the philosophy of, "I could have done this, I should have done that." This accomplishes nothing. You are in the present, and you are concerned about the future. You can't spend negative energy thinking about the past.

The First Day of the Rest of Your Life

I tell my clients when they come in, that this is the beginning of the rest of their lives. There are two parties in any separation. In some cases, one is the individual who has already moved on. He or she has planned what was going to happen in his or her life. The other party, "the one who was blindsided", to some degree at least, was not aware of the feelings of the other spouse to the point where he or she was ready to actually leave.

Marriages and relationships aren't perfect, and no one who's realistic should think that they are. However, things happen and there are situations where the parties grow apart, and one of the parties may not be as aware as the other as to what the feelings of the other spouse are until it is too late. However, once someone makes up their mind, there is no point in trying to waste energy in having them change their feelings, because only the individual is able to change the way they feel. Also, it is important to realize that negative energy and a negative person will bring down the positive person every time.

If there is negativity in your relationship, and it cannot be resolved, it is better for both parties, and where children are concerned, for their children to move on, because some people stay too long for the sake of their children. I was one of them.

What I have realized is that the happier you are, the happier your children will be, because one of your responsibilities as a parent is to teach your children what a good relationship is. It is not to stay in a bad relationship, and have them think that this is what they have to look forward to. You certainly are not helping either yourself or your children if you take that position.

Our Personal Experiences

One of the reasons we became Family Law attorneys is a result of our personal experiences in our own divorces. We wanted to help other people to make their separation as positive as possible. Along these lines, in any marriage, there are perceptions and misperceptions. No one is totally perfect in any situation, nor is the other person totally at fault. However, it really does not matter why the parties separate. What is important is that their separation does not adversely affect their children and their future relationships.

What is significant is that once someone realizes that they have made a mistake, whether it is after six months, five years, ten years, twenty years, that they at least act on it in a proactive manner. Do not have everyone in the relationship stay miserable, because that will not accomplish anything for anybody. If you are concerned about your children, you should give them what is considered to be a good example of what happiness is. In my case, I am now incredibly happily married, and my children from my prior marriage see that. They are happy for me and for themselves.

Fortunately, my three older children have met wonderful spouses so I now have two excellent sons-in-law and a great daughter-in-law. I am thrilled how happy they are, and hope that their marriages are as satisfying as my current marriage. Furthermore, I am blessed with having a fourteen year old daughter with my wife, who is the biggest blessing I could ever have imagined.

It is also important to note here that the new wife, as in my case, or new husband, has to be the type of person who loves your children. That is a prerequisite. If that is not the case, there is really no hope for your second marriage either. It is important and gratifying to see that my wife and my older children have a great relationship. My youngest daughter was the flower girl at both of my older daughters' weddings. She graduated to be a junior bridesmaid at my son's wedding.

I cannot adequately express the joy that I have when I see how well all of my children, as well as now my grandchildren, interact in an incredibly loving manner. Moreover, this is the hope for the future in any kind of separation, that there is a light at the end of the tunnel. Even though you may not have been happy during your first relationship, there is an excellent chance that you will be happy in the future. This is why you do not stagnate in a relationship that is not happy for the parties. It is good to forgive and forget, but it is also imperative to move on to create a new life.

I think that one of the great positives of our law firm is the fact that we are better attorneys because we were at one point clients. We understand much better what our clients now are going through, and have more compassion and empathy for them. My partner, who also was divorced, is now happily married with a wonderful wife and two little boys that are also the light of his life. I think our personal experience in divorce has helped us become better Family Law attorneys than those who have never had the experience of being divorced.

Chapter 2
Organized Effort

Written by Harvey L. Okun

For your separation to be successful you must have complete organized effort. Between attorney and client, organized effort is produced through the coordination of effort of two or more people, who work toward a definite end, in a spirit of harmony. It begins with total cooperation. Between spouses and significant others, extraordinary strength is shown by a person who can lay aside personal prejudices and move forward without friction from any individual with whom he or she is not in accord.

Organized Effort Can Take Many Forms

Mediation

Divorce mediation is about you and your soon to be ex deciding what is best for the both of you, and most importantly your children. Using the mediation strategy, you and your spouse meet with a neutral third party, the mediator.

With their help, you work through the issues you need to resolve, so the two of you may end your marriage as amicably and cost effectively as possible.

The issues covered include, but are not limited, to the following:

- Distribution of property
- Child custody and parenting time
- Child support and maintenance
- Retirement and taxes
- Finances

Sometimes agreements come easily, and other times mediating an agreement takes considerable effort. Mediators seek to keep the couple focused on relevant issues.

A divorce mediator is neutral and doesn't work for either party. That means the mediator can't give advice to either party. They must remain neutral no matter what the situation. Mediation is voluntary and continues only for so long as the mediator and the parties desire.

The length of mediation depends on what issues have been agreed to prior to mediation and those that still must be addressed at mediation. The time spent can be reduced if you and your spouse can come to agreements prior to the mediation process.

On average, mediation can be completed in 4 to 10 sessions. However, every case is obviously different. Mediation is a coordinated, cooperative effort, and when children are involved, it is about doing things in the best interest of the children.

Collaborative Law

Another example of organized effort is called collaborative law. Collaborative law is a relatively new way to resolve disputes by removing the disputed matter from the litigious courtroom setting and treating the process as a way to trouble shoot and problem solve rather than to fight.

As part of the collaborative process, both parties retain separate attorneys whose job is to settle disputes. No one may go to court during the collaborative process. If that occurs, the collaborative process terminates, and both attorneys disqualify themselves from any further involvement in the case. Each party signs a contractual agreement to honestly and openly disclose all documents and information relating to all the issues. Neither party may take advantage of a miscalculation or inadvertent mistakes.

Each party agrees to act respectfully and avoid disparaging or vilifying any of the participants. Insulating children is part of the process. All participants must act in such a way as to minimize the impact of the divorce on the children. The parties agree to implement outside experts where necessary in a cooperative fashion and share the cost related to those experts. Such experts are: real estate appraisers, business appraisers, accountants, and parenting consultants.

The primary goal of the process is to work toward an amicable solution and create a win-win situation for all. Neither party may seek or threaten court action to resolve disputes. If the parties decide to go to court as previously stated, the attorneys must withdraw, and the process begins anew in the court system.

One of the biggest differences in the collaborative process is that it recognizes emotional issues that exist that cannot be addressed by the legal system. The collaborative process addresses these issues by bringing them to the forefront and using outside experts described above as part of a team to find solutions.

When children are involved, the child specialist plays a very important role in the collaborative process. The child specialist works with children of divorcing parents. It is their job to assist the children's understanding that the parental dispute is not their fault and to teach them how to cope and communicate with their parents. This way the children have a voice in the process.

Four-Way Conferences

Collaborative law, like everything else, will not work in every case. It takes four willing participants. As good as collaborative law is, four-way conferences can also be equally successful and less expensive as the collaborative process, in that they do not restrict the participants in the same manner. Collaborative law requires paid experts in various fields. Four-way conferences can be done without experts, and be successful, as long as the parties are civil to each other, and try to work for a solution which is best for the parties and their children.

In a break-up, no one feels like a winner after it is over. The question which needs to be answered affirmatively is: "Did I accomplish my primary goals?"

Our Philosophy

We believe that these are the correct priorities and handle cases in this fashion. Where children are involved, look out for the children first. However, we never ignore in any way the financial priorities of our clients. Obviously the finances are extremely important, but human beings always come first.

Whatever method that you choose, whether it be collaborative law, mediation, or four-way conferences between the parties and their lawyers, it is paramount that you maintain organized efforts. Only through organized effort will all of the parties accomplish their goals.

Chapter 3
Confidentiality—Your Secret is Safe

Written by Harvey L. Okun

"We have two ears and one mouth so that we can listen twice as much as we speak." Epictetus

Confidentiality serves the purpose of encouraging clients to speak frankly and with full disclosure to their attorneys about their cases.

Full disclosure helps to ensure that lawyers will be able to carry out their duty through zealous representation and avoids unnecessary surprises by opposing counsel, which may weaken the client's position. Also, a distrustful client might hide a relevant fact which he or she thinks is incriminating, but which a skilled lawyer could turn to the client's advantage.

Trust is a Gateway to Opening Lines of Communication.

A valuable lesson for client and attorney is to listen carefully and speak only when necessary. It is important that the client has trust for the attorney, and also that the attorney has trust in the client in order for the relationship to be successful. This trust factor will prevent any surprises in the courtroom. It is very important that an individual who comes in to see an attorney develops a bond of trust so they can disclose everything that is relevant to their case.

The Successful Mortgage Broker

A young lady came in to my office for a consultation. We spoke for an hour, and we went through all of the questions I generally ask a potential client to see what his or her goals were with respect to the divorce. At this initial consultation, I make sure that they are compatible with me in terms of their goals and the manner in which we will accomplish their goals. In this particular case, this young lady was a successful mortgage broker. At the end of our meeting, she retained me to handle her divorce case.

The next morning she called to inform me that there was something very important that she had not divulged. She said that she needed to see me in person to discuss it. She came in and told me something that was somewhat shocking and surprising. She obviously had developed a trust in me during that first hour of consultation so that she was able to tell me something that was not easy for her to divulge.

She told me that her three boys were not the children of her husband even though he thought that they were. This communication obviously created a major confidentiality dilemma for me, the attorney. I could not allow this factual information to ever be divulged to opposing counsel. The husband certainly could not find out, and most importantly, my client certainly did not want the children to find out. My client also did not want to hurt her husband financially.

Since she didn't want her husband to have to pay child support, it was helpful that she earned an annual income of three hundred thousand dollars, and he was a mechanic earning fifty thousand dollars a year.

In order to offset the child support which he would normally be required to pay, we worked out an arrangement where even though she had primary physical custody, he waived the alimony to which he was entitled in exchange for not having to pay child support. By resolving this case in such a manner, the confidentiality was kept, and no one was hurt in this situation emotionally or economically. This story demonstrates that it is of paramount importance that the client trust the attorney to tell him or her everything.

Chapter 4

Preserving the One Resource You Can Never Get Back–Your Time

Written by Alan L. Billian

"Time is the coin of your life. It is the only coin you have, and only you can determine how it will be spent. Be careful lest you let other people spend it for you." Carl Sandburg

Since you are now faced with the prospect, either voluntarily or involuntarily, of splitting up with your spouse or significant other, what do you do next? First, decide what's important to you. Do you want to spend the next few years mired in litigation, or do you want to focus on a prompt resolution of your issues, whether they are custody and support related, financial related, or property related?

How important to you is your time? Do you work full time? Are you a stay-at-home-parent? How do you spend your days? What is the value of your time to you? The time you spend mired in litigation is time you can spend doing almost anything else.

Time Management

There is one skill that every person needs to learn; it's called time management. When mastered, it can lead to great success. Ignore it, and it can lead to failure.

How do you master the skill of time management as it relates to your divorce, separation, or custody case?

A. <u>Set realistic goals</u>: Want to see positive results quickly? Set realistic and specific goals on a daily basis. Write them down and cross them off when they are completed. Start with the most difficult ones first. What is most important to you? Make sure your lawyer knows this, and make sure you and your lawyer are on the same page with your goals. This allows for both of you to be focused on the right issues and to have organized effort.

B. <u>Respond to all of your lawyer's requests without delay</u>: Know that whatever information your lawyer asks you for is important and is being requested for a specific reason. If documents are requested, get those documents together as fast as possible. Be over-inclusive and not under-inclusive. Let your lawyer decide what is important, and what is not. If your lawyer has questions for you, and he or she will, be open and honest. Holding something back can lead to disaster. Openness and honesty allows for you and your lawyer to better plan and strategize, and to work more efficiently. It's like the old saying "the best offense is a good defense."

C. <u>Make meetings more efficient</u>: If you are going to a meeting with your lawyer, or even having a telephone conference, write out a list of questions that you need answered. Know going into that meeting or telephone conference what you want to achieve.

D. <u>Stay Focused</u>: There is no magic pill to success in your case. Stay focused on accomplishing the tasks that will generate the results you desire.

E. <u>Avoid procrastination on the most difficult tasks</u>: Attack the most difficult tasks first instead of overanalyzing them. Don't let the paralysis of fear set in. If you spend too much time thinking about an unpleasant task, you'll avoid accomplishing it, and you'll waste time worrying.

Use Your Time Wisely

"If you don't have the time to do it right, when will you have the time to do it over?" John Wooden

Remember time is your most important resource and can never be recovered. Once it's gone, it's gone. Time is not infinite. So again, the goal should be to proceed through the process without wasting unnecessary time.

Take the case of Larry who had been married for more than thirty years. In addition to raising children, Larry and his wife had spent their marriage becoming financially comfortable by acquiring houses, vehicles, the personal property to fill those houses, and investment, bank, and retirement accounts.

Larry and his wife had drifted apart over the years, and they decided it was time to separate and to get a divorce. Before either of them had filed for divorce, Larry and his wife hired separate attorneys, with Larry hiring Okun/Billian.

Larry and his wife, with attorneys present, met in our office in what at first blush appeared to be a four-way conference for purposes of attempting to negotiate an amicable settlement. Larry's wife made a "take it or leave it" settlement demand and refused to negotiate further. Larry crossed his arms and said "no, this has to be a negotiation if this is going to work." The meeting was over.

Shortly after that meeting, Larry made a counter-proposal which was immediately rejected by his wife. A divorce complaint was filed by her, and a counter-complaint was filed by Larry.

25

The parties spent the next two and a half years, going through the discovery process (seeking proof of factual allegations made by each other as well as seeking documentary evidence to support those allegations). Motions were filed, along with oppositions to those motions, court hearings ensued, trial dates were picked and postponed, and settlement conferences were scheduled, postponed and rescheduled.

Finally, after two and a half years, the parties attended a settlement conference, and Larry's wife made a settlement demand which was the same demand that she made two and a half years earlier. Larry countered that demand, and with the assistance of a retired judge, a settlement was reached. The settlement that was reached left Larry's wife with less than the amount that she had demanded two and a half years earlier.

What the case had cost Larry, in addition to tens of thousands of dollars in legal fees, was his time. His life had been on stand-still for that entire period of time. He now had a girlfriend, but couldn't move on with his life, because he was still married to his wife for two and a half years longer than necessary. He was stuck thinking about his divorce case every single day, because he couldn't put it behind him. In addition to his full time job, he had a second full time job, which was fighting with his wife and her attorney.

Had Larry made the decision to settle initially, his new life would have started years earlier. He had lost the time that he could never get back.

The moral of this story is simple: decide where to pick your battles and what is important. Create a game plan: what do you want to accomplish, and how do you get it? Create a strategy with your lawyer, and stick to it as best you can. This is where organized effort comes in. Can you get what you want without spending a lot of time to get it? If so, resolve your case and your issues and move on if it's possible.

"Time is the most precious resource that you have, so treat it as such."
Mark Luterman, CEO, Small Business Secret Weapon Company

Chapter 5
Protecting Your Children

Written by Harvey L. Okun and Alan L. Billian

"The most precious jewels you'll ever have around your neck are the arms of your children." Unknown

We have been fortunate in our careers to have won custody cases for many devoted parents.

Two-State Custody Fight - by Harvey L. Okun

There is one dad who has a special place in my heart. He has five children aged, at the time of his custody fight, 16, 12, 10, 8 and 7. Dad is a consultant for the Department of Defense and lives in Maryland. Even though he had separated from his wife in March of 2010, he was not divorced, and there had been no custody orders in any court at the time of the custody litigation.

As much as he loved his children at the time of separation, he felt that the children, who were much younger at the time, would be better off with their mother, who lived in Washington State. However, when his children came to visit him in Maryland during the summer of 2011, the second and third oldest children expressed their feelings. They wanted to stay permanently with dad.

The oldest child had already left Washington in August 2011. The oldest kids explained to dad that they were used by their mother as babysitters. The mother would go out at 6 pm without preparing their dinner, and she would not come back until after they left for school the following morning. Also, according to the children, she did not help them with their homework. Most importantly, they explained that she did not show affection towards them.

What made the case even more difficult was the fact it was governed under the Uniform Custody Act ("UCA"). The UCA requires a child to be a resident of a state for six months prior to a court obtaining jurisdiction. Applying that statute to this case, Washington State had jurisdiction over the four youngest children, with Maryland having jurisdiction for the oldest child. I was fortunate to find an incredibly talented attorney to represent my client in Washington State, and I represented him in Maryland.

After many long, arduous months, I am extremely happy to report that Dad gained custody of all five children. His oldest recently received a full scholarship to a great school where she is majoring in marine biology. The rest of his "fab five" have also excelled in their respective schools as well. It takes a special dad to give up his personal life for the benefit of his children. This is why this dad will always have a special place in my heart.

Best Interests of the Child

In making an initial custody determination, judges are charged with determining what is in a particular child's or the children's best interests. Some factors which judges are required to use are:

1) fitness of the parents;
2) character and reputation of the parties;
3) desire of the natural parents and agreements between the parties;
4) potentiality of maintaining natural family relations;
5) preference of the child;
6) material opportunities affecting the future life of the child;

7) age, health and sex of the child;
8) residences of parents and opportunity for visitation;
9) length of separation from the natural parents;
10) prior voluntary abandonment or surrender;
11) sincerity of the parents' requests for custody, and the willingness to share custody; and
12) the children's success in their current environment.

Generally, judges will not weigh any one factor to the exclusion of all others.

My Favorite Foster Mom - by Harvey L. Okun

One of the most gratifying accomplishments in my career was to convince the court to award a foster mother physical and legal custody of her foster children, whom she subsequently adopted.

The mother in this case gave birth to two girls minutes apart. What was amazing was that the two girls had two different DNA profiles, meaning that they had two different fathers. The birth mother had accused more than ten men of being potential fathers. None of them were! After removing the children from their mother's care, the Baltimore City Department of Social Services placed the children with a wonderful lady (my client) who became their foster mother.   Unfortunately in Maryland, foster parents have limited, if any, legal rights. Therefore, it was necessary to prepare a "Motion To Intervene" in this matter, which would allow her to participate as a party in the legal proceedings. After a grueling two-day trial, the Judge issued the following opinion:

"There is no perfect solution to this case. The court is required to weigh the legal preference and also to apply the standard in the best interests of the children. The best interests of the children is that they have security, which is the feeling of safety as well as the actual aspect of being safe; that they be in a loving environment and that this be a stable environment."

The judge in this case ruled that the children's best interests were served by my client who had no biological relationship to them. It is heartwarming to know that there are people who have the capacity to love someone else's children as if they were their own. For this reason, this client will always be special to me.

The Story of Bonnie—by Alan L. Billian

My client, Amy, was married to a gentleman named Dave with whom she raised three lovely children. During the course of their marriage Dave had a brief affair and fathered a daughter; Bonnie. Amy told Dave, "bring her into our home and I'll raise her as my own," and they did with little or no contact from Bonnie's natural mother.

When Bonnie was eight years old, Dave died suddenly. Knowing that Dave's death would result in a social security check for Bonnie, Bonnie's natural mother surfaced and filed a Complaint for Custody, attempting to take custody of Bonnie away from Amy. After numerous court appearances, an attorney being appointed to represent the best interests of Bonnie, and a full day trial, Amy was awarded custody of Bonnie. Bonnie went on to finish school, get a job and to eventually become a wonderful mother herself, all due to the influence of Amy, who was not her natural mother and who had no blood relationship to Bonnie.

In finding in her favor, the judge determined that the ties that bound Bonnie and Amy were stronger than the blood that tied Bonnie to her natural mother, and that these exceptional circumstances weighed in favor of Amy being awarded custody.

The reason why Amy has a special place in my heart is that she had every reason to be bitter, to be angry, to turn her back on Bonnie and she didn't. She knew that Bonnie needed her, and needed a strong family in her corner. She knew that Bonnie's best interests were more important than her own. As a result of that case, and my relationship with Amy, I have been treated like a member of the family. I have been at weddings, and unfortunately some funerals, but Amy and her family will always be near and dear to me.

The Story of Grayson—by Alan L. Billian

Several years ago, I represented a young man named John. When I met John, he was about 19 years old and had fathered a child with a young lady a few years younger. They hid the pregnancy from friends and family. Shortly after the birth of a baby boy, Grayson, they married and moved in with John's family in Baltimore. A few years later, John's wife, Grayson's mother, met a man over the internet and created a scheme to leave John, and to take Grayson away with her.

When John was working, she packed up Grayson and took off with the new man and left for Canada. She left a note saying she was leaving with Grayson and not coming back. John and his mother called the police and had an Amber Alert issued. The mother was apprehended with Grayson at the Canadian border, and Grayson was turned over to John.

After an emergency court hearing, Grayson was turned over to the mother, because the judge did not find that the mother had placed Grayson in any danger. John then fired the attorney that represented him, and hired me.

Over the next two years, the mother refused to allow John to exercise any additional time with Grayson beyond the court ordered "every other weekend" visitation. She denied every request for additional time, even when it was for special birthdays, and John's family events. She refused to allow John to take Grayson's clothes for visits, refused to tell him where Grayson was going for pediatric visits and did everything possible to cut him out of Grayson's life, but John refused to give up.

He never stopped asking for additional time and never went away. He persisted at every opportunity, even when it was clear that the answer would always be "no." Grayson's mother concocted stories of abuse and mental illness - anything she could think of as a way to stop John from seeing Grayson. She even decided to move to Canada and was planning on taking Grayson away from John, his family and her family, and took the position that she was the only person in Grayson's life who mattered.

After two days of trial and after relentless cross-examination by me, John was awarded full legal and physical custody of Grayson. His battle was finally over. Grayson could live with his dad every day. It was the happiest day of John's life and one of my proudest moments as a lawyer.

A few days later, I sent a gift to Grayson along with the following letter:

"Dear Grayson,

My name is Alan Billian. I met your Dad and Grandma Candy and Grandpa Bob almost two years ago in July of 2008, when they came to me and asked me for help. Your mother had taken you to live with her, and they only got to see you for a few days every few weeks. All they wanted was for you to get to spend more time with them. They were used to seeing you every day, and they missed you terribly. They were so sad that they did not get to see you more.

Since the time that I first met your Dad and grandparents, they asked me to try to get them permission to spend more time with you. They called me all of the time. They loved the time you got to spend with them, but they wanted more and more. It was very important to them that they get to help you grow up and learn to do things like talking, reading books, playing games and riding a bike. They dreamed of being able to have you wake up in their homes for more than just a few days each month. No matter what anyone else may have told you when you were living with your mother, your Dad and grandparents never stopped loving you or caring about you or thinking about you. They are good people who love you very much and always will.

Last week your Dad and grandparents got their wish. A Judge gave them everything they ever wanted and dreamed. He told them that you would live with them and spend most of your time with them. They would get to help you grow up and learn to do all of the things that Dads like to do with their boys and that grandparents like to do with their grandsons. Your Aunt Amy was so happy that she told all of her friends that she thought she was dreaming, but she woke up and it was real; you were back with your family where you belonged. Your whole family gave me lots of hugs for helping them make their dreams come true.

Your Dad told me that you like the movie "Cars" a lot. My boys like it too. They helped me pick out the enclosed gift for you. I hope you like it.

Your friend,
Alan L. Billian"

Chapter 6
Preserving a Lifetime of Assets

Written by Alan L. Billian

"Your greatest asset is your earning ability. Your greatest resource is your time." Brian Tracy

You have been working for your entire adulthood, and you have your earnings, and if you are lucky have put together some savings, retirement assets, real estate and personal property. You are now faced with a break up, with or without a divorce. If you are not married, your personal income is at stake. If you are married, in addition to your personal income, you have the assets that you have managed to put together over the years. So what happens next? What are the considerations?

If you have minor children involved, you want to do right by them and make sure they are supported and that their needs are being met. If you are married and there are property issues, you want to make sure that you don't give up more than you need to, or receive as much as you are entitled to receive. How do you accomplish that?

First of all, tell your lawyer everything, and leave nothing out. Let your lawyer decide what facts or details are important and what are not. Second, tell your lawyer what you want. If there are items of property that were yours before the marriage, let your lawyer know. If there were gifts given to you by your spouse, let your lawyer know. If there is something that is so important to you that you consider it a deal breaker, let your lawyer know.

On the other hand, if something tangible means nothing to you, let your lawyer know. Additionally, know the costs involved in taking any particular course of action.

"By fighting you never get enough, but by yielding you get more than you expected." Dale Carnegie, <u>How to Win Friends and Influence People</u>

<u>Is it Really Worth it?</u>

Many years ago I went through a divorce and found myself fighting over a camera. The divorce lawyer asked, "do you want to pay me $200 per hour to fight over a $150 camera, or do you want to buy a new one?" My answer? "I'll buy a new one."

When I opened my solo practice, I met an attorney who had been working for decades handling divorce cases. We were in court for the beginning of a two day divorce trial involving custody, child support and property issues. We were ultimately able to settle the case before the trial began. As we were chatting, she relayed to me the following story: Once she was representing a client in a divorce case, the parties and their lawyers had spent several hours in the courthouse on the day of trial negotiating a settlement and reached an impasse over a set of kitchen canisters. Both parties wanted that set, and neither was willing to give in. The parties took a lunch break, and the attorney went to "Bed, Bath and Beyond" and purchased the identical set of canisters and returned with them to the courthouse. She took them out of the bag and showed them to the parties to let them know that there was nothing that stood in the way of completing the settlement. There was only one problem, actually two problems, the parties! Both of them wanted the canister set that had been in the marital home, and neither wanted the new set. It took the judge to convince the parties to settle.

Was it worth it? In my opinion, definitely not. To those parties? Maybe, but probably not. Not when they had time to step back and think about it. Did either of them really win anything significant by fighting over those canisters? Absolutely not.

It's Just Stuff

Years ago, I represented a gentleman named Ron. Ron and his wife had spent decades acquiring rental properties in Maryland. When it came time to divorce, Ron's wife demanded, and she was entitled to half of those properties. Ron made a list of the properties and made a proposal on how to divide them up based on their respective values, those with mortgages and those without. When his wife objected to part of his proposed split, he pulled me aside and said "Alan, it's just stuff; I can always acquire more stuff. Let her take the ones she wants, and I'll take what's left." While that was going to an extreme, the point made sense - if you have no sentimental attachment to it, it's harder to fight about it.

If you do want to fight for it, how much do you want to fight? Is it worth going to trial or not? If you are willing to go to trial over it, it better be valuable, either financially or emotionally.

Do the Math

Sometimes it's easy to do the math: What is this item worth used, and what will it cost me to replace it? How much do I anticipate paying my lawyer to fight over it for me?

Jointly Titled Property

While there are exceptions to the rule, generally courts will not transfer jointly titled property from one party to the other. Instead, if the item of property you are fighting over has a certificate of title, and that item is jointly titled, the court will likely order it sold and the proceeds divided. If you don't want that to happen, you might need to give up something else to get it and prevent it from being sold by the court.

What Are You Really Fighting For?

Another thing that you need to ask yourself is: "are you simply fighting for the sake of fighting?" Do you really want *that* asset, or do you really want to conquer your spouse or significant other? More often than not, it's not about the material object, it's about the desire to be the victor. If it is more about winning, let it go. Is it worth the stress of fighting? Is it worth making yourself sick to continue the fight? Is it worth the negative energy that you are spending engaging in the fight? In the long run, this fight that you are engaging in becomes all-consuming and costs more than taking the high road would have cost in terms of emotional energy and long-term happiness. Do what's right, and the reward is tenfold!

Chapter 7
Hiring the Right Lawyer

Written by Alan L. Billian

"Discourage litigation. Persuade your neighbors to compromise whenever you can. Point out to them how the nominal winner is often a real loser---in fees, expenses, and waste of time. As a peacemaker the lawyer has a superior opportunity of being a good [person]. There will still be business enough." Abraham Lincoln

Friends, colleagues and arm chair quarterbacks will tell you that you need to find the most aggressive lawyer, one who will take a scorched earth position and will fight on every point for you. Resist them, ignore them, and think about what your goals are!

<u>Definiteness of Purpose</u>

If you don't have a definiteness of purpose, that is, knowing exactly what it is you want, you will lose sight of the end result of your desired achievement. Ultimately, you'll experience a lack of success and be dissatisfied with the outcome.

Success depends upon organized effort, and the first step of achieving organized effort is to create a definiteness of purpose. Creating this purpose will help you concentrate and focus on any particular task until you have mastered it.

Your goals are to protect yourself and your children, preserve your mental health, your hard earned wealth, and your time. A lawyer who fights for the sake of fighting will not take into account any of your goals. These attorneys are ego driven, or worse, driven to make as much money as possible out of your particular dispute, without regard for what you really want. That lawyer will tell you: "Don't worry about anything; just let me do my job." That's not the lawyer you want to hire.

Recently, I met with a woman who confirmed this exact idea. She needed my representation in her divorce case. She told me that I was the second lawyer she had met with. The first lawyer told her not to worry about anything, and just let him do his job, and everything would be fine. She did not want to be treated in this manner and wanted to be actively involved in her case. She got the impression that the first lawyer would not let that happen. She is now our client.

You want a lawyer who knows his or her way around a courtroom. You don't want a lawyer who only wants to negotiate and settle every case, who doesn't know enough to know when a good deal is in front them. Your lawyer will have no negotiating power for you if that lawyer has a reputation for settling everything. A good lawyer knows when they can work towards a negotiated settlement. A good lawyer also knows when they need to push.

Recently, I had the displeasure of handling my client's divorce and custody case where the lawyer who represented my client's wife had no experience in handling divorce and custody cases. As a result of his inexperience, he had created completely unrealistic expectations in his client. We spent an entire day working with a judge in trying to negotiate a settlement. After six hours, an agreement was reached - or so I thought. As we were finalizing the agreement with the judge, the wife began to question the fairness of the deal, the amount of alimony she would be paid, the monetary award to be paid to her, and the specific items of property she would receive. The agreement fell apart, and a trial date was scheduled.

After the trial, which took place three months later, my client was granted full custody of his daughter, and the wife received significantly less alimony and a small monetary award. That inexperienced lawyer cost his client tens of thousands of dollars.

Deal Breakers

Harvey and I recently attended a meeting between our client and his long time business partner. While this was a business partnership, and not a marriage, there are similarities to a break-up in either situation. These two gentlemen had finally decided that a break up was necessary because they had lost trust in one another. The meeting was for the sole purpose of trying to wind down a business they had been involved in, and our client's partner felt that our client owed him money. Our client came to the meeting with a person who was interested in making a deal to continue to operate the business. Our client's former partner hired an attorney who wanted to call all of the shots. He had no interest in negotiating and trying to reach a compromise, even though the purpose of the meeting was to attempt to reach an agreement. Instead of negotiating and looking for a compromise, the meeting ended after 15 minutes.

When we walked out of the office, our client commented that his former partner had hired a "deal breaker, and not a deal maker." As a result of hiring a "deal breaker," that person cost himself thousands of dollars.

Stirring Things Up to Create a Fight

Several years ago, a client engaged my services for the purpose of drafting and negotiating a pre-nuptial agreement with his fiancée several weeks before they were to marry. My client was looking to preserve his business interests that he had created in the decade or so before he was to get married. I prepared a draft of the agreement, which he gave to his fiancée with whom he lived.

My client's fiancée hired an attorney who was ego driven and enamored with himself. He saw every client as an opportunity for a fight. That lawyer called my client's fiancée and said, "you won't believe how your fiancé is trying to take advantage of you; you can't let him do this." That lawyer was attempting to create a fight between this couple a few weeks before their wedding. Luckily my client and his fiancée ignored the lawyer's attempt to create a fight, and a compromise was reached.

The Story of Harvey and Alan

In 2005, I received a phone call from a gentleman who lived out of state and had received a complaint for divorce from his wife's attorney. After an extensive telephone consultation, he engaged my services.

When he sent me the paperwork, there was insufficient time to prepare and file an answer in a timely fashion. I sent an email to the wife's attorney, Harvey Okun, and asked for an extension of time. The response? "Okay, but you'll owe me." Little did I know that I would still owe him today! That case was as acrimonious as a case could have been. There were children involved and financial issues; there was a marital home with lots of equity.

Everything that there could have been a dispute about was disputed.

Harvey and I each subpoenaed the records that we needed (compelling a non-party to produce documents), issued discovery (written questions directed to the parties seeking documents, and the factual and legal basis for the positions each side had been taking). Harvey and I had positioned our clients so that we were each ready to litigate our clients' claims, but were fully informed with the knowledge necessary to negotiate a settlement.

We spent the better part of a morning and part of an afternoon with our clients and a mediator negotiating a settlement that benefitted our clients and their children. Harvey and I saw our clients' goals, and understood what each of our clients wanted to get out of their case. We saw there was a family that hung in the balance, and a negotiated resolution was better than a courtroom showdown.

The point of this story is that you need a lawyer who can strike that delicate balance between being aggressive and being conciliatory. What Harvey and I learned about each other was that we treated our clients and our cases exactly the same way. We were both able to find the balance between being aggressive and conciliatory, and to work for the best interests of our clients without regard to our personal gain. We respected each other so much that we joined forces as partners six years later. A true success story!

Afterward

Like anyone else who works for a living, sometimes we wake up and ask ourselves "why do we do what we do for a living?" And then you receive a letter like the one you are about to read.

"Hello Attorney Okun:

I am writing this letter to thank you for all that you have done for my son and me. I found your name in the yellow pages and it was a blessing that I did. I was going through a difficult time in my life. I was going through a nasty divorce. In the middle of the divorce my son ran away from an abusive relationship with his mother. He was failing school and was a very angry young man. You helped me get my divorce and to obtain full custody of my son. You were more like a friend than an attorney. You gave me a chance to raise my son and to help change his life. He is now in college and working. He is doing great things in his life and I owe a big part of that to you. I thank you for everything, and for giving me an opportunity to raise my son. You are a great attorney and a great friend.

THANK YOU,
CP"

And then we realize, for us, we do what we do because we have the capacity to help people and to change their lives forever. That is a great reason to wake up every day and go to work.

About The Authors

A University of Maryland alumnus, Harvey L. Okun has been in private general practice for more than 30 years. Harvey L. Okun was admitted to practice by the Supreme Court of the United States and the Court of Appeals of Maryland, as well as Baltimore City and all counties in every jurisdiction in the State of Maryland. Prior to entering his private practice, Harvey L. Okun was counsel to the US Army Corps of Engineers, and was counsel for the School Board of Baltimore City and the Community College of Baltimore. On September 1, 2011 Harvey joined with his friend and protégé Alan L. Billian to form Okun/Billian PA.

Harvey serves as a board member and an attorney for Casey Cares Foundation; a not for profit organization that assists children and their families deal with life threatening medical conditions. He also serves as a volunteer attorney for Jewish Legal Services as well as an attorney for The Defender of Animal Rights.

A University of Baltimore alumnus, Alan L. Billian has been in private practice for more than 22 years. Alan was admitted to practice by the Court of Appeals of Maryland in December 1991, the United States District Court for the District of Maryland in July 1993, and practices in all counties in every jurisdiction in the State of Maryland.

Before forming Okun/Billian PA, Alan began his law practice as an Associate Attorney with the Law Offices of Cooper, Beckman & Tuerk concentrating in the areas of Asbestos and General Civil Litigation, including Divorce and Family Law and Personal Injury Law. Alan left Cooper, Beckman & Tuerk in March 1995 and opened the Law Office of Alan L. Billian, PC on April 1, 1995 where his practice areas included Divorce, Custody and Family Law, Criminal Law, Consumer Bankruptcy, Estate Planning and Administration, Corporate Law and Business Litigation. Alan merged his practice on November 1, 1999 to form the firm of Schnitzer, Segall, Hymer & Billian, LLC where he continued to practice until August 31, 2011 when he joined his friend and mentor, Harvey L. Okun, to create the firm of Okun/Billian PA.

Alan has also served as a volunteer board member of several neighborhood associations and regularly handles pro bono cases from several local agencies that provide legal services to those who cannot afford to hire attorneys.